Shave Your Head:

A Female Ranger Graduate Answers
Your Questions

Erin McShane

Contents

The Ranger Creed

Recognizing that I volunteered as a Ranger, fully knowing the hazards of my chosen profession, I will always endeavor to uphold the prestige, honor, and high esprit de corps of the Rangers.

Acknowledging the fact that a Ranger is a more elite Soldier who arrives at the cutting edge of battle by land, sea, or air, I accept the fact that as a Ranger my country expects me to move further, faster and fight harder than any other Soldier.

Never shall I fail my comrades. I will always keep myself mentally alert, physically strong and morally straight and I will shoulder more than my share of the task whatever it may be, one-hundred-percent and then some.

Gallantly will I show the world that I am a specially selected and well-trained Soldier. My courtesy to superior officers, neatness of dress and care of equipment shall set the example for others to follow.

Energetically will I meet the enemies of my country. I shall defeat them on the field of battle for I am better trained and will fight with all my might. Surrender is not a Ranger word. I will never leave a fallen comrade to fall into the hands of the enemy and under no circumstances will I ever embarrass my country.

Readily will I display the intestinal fortitude required to fight on to the Ranger objective and complete the mission though I be the lone survivor.

Rangers lead the way!

Introduction

Why. This is where it all begins. What is your *why?* For you: Why do you want to go to Ranger School? For me: Why do I write this book? This book is a way for me to give back and say 'thank you.' Thank you to my countless mentors, my family, my friends, and even random strangers who supported me. To my bosses, who let me take time away and the peers and subordinates who covered for me. Thank you, Mom, for your encouraging letters. Thank you to the Ranger instructor who helped me recover equipment that had moved on to Florida phase without me. Though I can't do the same for you as you did for me, I can support the next generation of students who are capable, motivated, and could use some encouragement.

This is not a comprehensive guide book for Ranger School. Instead, this book gives insight into Ranger School through the lens of my experience. The book is useful for any Ranger candidate, but some of the information applies more to women than to men. This is not because of any personal bias. It is because there are many female Ranger candidates who don't have access to female graduates. Many of these candidates are curious about a female Ranger's experience and how that experience may be relevant to their own training.

Soon after graduating Ranger School in December 2017, I was asked to speak at the United States Military Academy, West Point. There was no way I could refuse. As the officer in charge of the Sapper Train-Up program for the Army Engineer Schoolhouse and as an instructor at the Basic Officer Course (the first professional Army Course for second lieutenants) I had already had the chance to answer questions for lieutenants preparing for Sapper and Ranger Schools. Speaking at West Point was another chance to help Ranger candidates prepare for the challenges ahead. At the academy, I jumped from one engagement to the next and then had dinner with the cadets. West Point's main dining facility is enormous. Designed to feed over 4,000 cadets, family style, all at once, the massive hall is filled with wooden tables for ten and capped by cathedral ceilings. After dinner, some cadets approached me to ask questions. One short freshman hung around once the small crowd of curious cadets had dissipated. She looked up at me and asked, "What was your Army Physical Fitness Test (APFT) score as a cadet?" I understood the intent of the question: She wasn't asking for raw numbers; she was asking whether I was relatable or not. She wanted to know whether she was comparable to me, whether I was normal, or if I'd made it through Ranger training because of some Herculean abilities. I knew what she meant, because I'd been in her shoes.

A year before, 26 years old and a first lieutenant, I'd scoured the internet for any and every data point I could find on the only three female Ranger graduates to that point. I wanted to know everything. Were they Olympic-level athletes? What had their training been? Was there specific training I needed because I was a woman? What were their stories? What was it like for them to go through such a famously rigorous school? What was difficult, challenging, unique? Intuitively, I knew I could make it through. Cognitively, I wanted confirmation. With her APFT question, this cadet confirmed that I was not the only one who spent hours in search of what it is like, and whether, as a woman, I could make it through. This book seeks to answer a few of these questions for those who are still scouring the internet.

There are countless capable soldiers who just want one piece of information. That one piece that will boost their confidence so they *know* beyond a shadow of a doubt that they can, and will, make it through Ranger School. I'm sorry. I don't have that information for you. No one does. No one has 100% confidence either. What I **do** have is a story; something you may be able to relate to and answers to some of your questions. In this Q & A-style book, I've answered the most common questions I get from young women and men interested in Ranger training. For instance, are the standards the same? Yes, for everyone. What was the hardest part? Endurance. Where should I focus my training? On the requirements, or 'gates,' of Ranger School, your weaknesses, and on gaining external, expert feedback. This is the same for men and women. The most common question from both men and women, civilians and soldiers: What was it like to shave your head? Honestly, it was like a massage, stripping away pretenses and helping me blend in.

Before we start, I should make clear that I am not a true Ranger, meaning I am not a member of Ranger Regiment. I should also say, I was not a stellar Ranger student as it took me two 'recycles' to learn some lessons. I am not Infantry, either. I am an Engineer, ESSAYONS! (Essayons, by the way, is French for 'let us try,' or in other words, 'hold my beer.') I was deliberate in learning everything I could to pass Ranger School. I felt I had to be deliberate in order to pass. All efforts paid off.

I am the 9th female to graduate Ranger School, the 2nd double tab: e.g., the second woman to graduate both Sapper and Ranger schools. I am normal. I am no different from the thousands of students who graduated Ranger School before me—I just look different. I promise to answer all questions as truthfully as I can in hopes that you may glean some lesson that proves useful. If this book helps one person, then it is a success. As you go through the book, treat it as a choose your own adventure book. Pick the questions which interest you, ignore the ones which don't.

Lastly, if you have questions you want answered, the luxury of a digital book is that it can always be updated. Email me at syhquestions@gmail.com. You may find your question answered in the next edition, or on femaleranger.com. Also, there is a wealth of information and advice from female ranger graduates on the Ranger School Candidates Facebook page: https://www.facebook.com/groups/rangerschoolcandidates.

1.

What was it like to shave your head?

Why is hair such a big deal? I'll never know. Some women tie a lot of meaning to their hair. I can appreciate that. It boosts attractiveness, helping in personal and professional interactions. It takes a long time to grow back, so a woman can't decide it looks bad and get long hair the next day.

I didn't know that the buzz cut was a requirement until well after I'd committed to attending the Ranger Training Assessment Course (RTAC). At the time, there was just one Ranger class, a pilot class, that was open to women. After that, the gates to Ranger training could be flung wide open for women, or shut for another 50 years. No one knew. Not a year prior, I had heard a rumor that Ranger School was working on admitting women. Ranger School had called Sapper School, asking how to integrate. I was not privy to the conversation. In my mind, though, Sapper School hardly had a response. They'd integrated in 1999, years before the Sapper Instructors themselves had tabbed. "Treat them like Soldiers," they said, "just like everyone else." After joining my first unit, my company commander approached me. I hadn't told anyone at my new unit that I intended to go to Ranger School. "Erin, I don't know if or when Ranger

School is going to open to women. When it does, I want to send you. You can make it through. You have what it takes." I'll never forget that conversation. Within months, Ranger School announced its pilot class. To enter the pilot class, women first had to pass RTAC.

My Battalion Sergeant Major was the one who told me. I believe he asked me, actually, "So, when are you going to cut your hair?" Was that a joke? No? Well, I'd always thought about cutting it short. I was just pretty sure I'd regret the decision within days. There would be no regret now. I went home to find my boyfriend in my living room, parked on his favorite gray couch. "Dan? I'm going to have to shave my head." God bless him. He didn't skip a beat. He jumped up from the couch, shouting, "We're going to be the cutest gay couple ever!"

Everything is more fun when there's competition involved, so I capitalized on the buzz cut. The rules of the game were as follows: whichever Soldier in my platoon increased their score the most from the diagnostic to the record fitness test was rewarded with the chance to shave my head. The soldier with the best overall score shaved my Platoon Sergeant's. My Battalion Sergeant Major even had his head shaved at the event as a show of support. These men were great leaders. Once buzzed, my head felt amazing. It was the first time I'd felt the breeze on my scalp. Every head touch felt like a massage. I took a picture and sent it to my sister. I remember thinking, this is me— no distraction, no hair. Just me, straight up.

Bathroom Jokes

Since my first buzz, short hair has been my status quo. Not by choice necessarily, it just didn't grow out before I entered Ranger School with buzz cut #2. It's been fun and funny to have short hair. When bald, let's just say I don't look like Natalie Portman. I look like a little boy. Like my little brother, in fact. When buying alcohol at the grocery store, I ask myself whether to hand over the 'boy' ID (buzz cut), or the 'girl' ID (flowing locks). Once, I asked this question aloud. The cashier had zero sense of humor and replied, "This isn't a beauty contest."

While hunting for project supplies in Home Depot, I hear a voice behind me, "Sir, can I help you?" Rather than address the mistake, I say, "Yes, please, I'm looking for X." The middle-aged saleswoman is rocking the same butch haircut I am. She's taken aback. "Oh my gosh, I just did to you what everyone does to me." (No offense taken, I promise.)

The Army gate guards are the most common offenders. "Good morning, Sir!" the guard says, scanning my identification card as my yellow Wrangler slows to a stop. Most people going on post, it seems, are male, so the odds are in their favor. The guard is on a roll; I'm not about to slow it. "Thank you, have a good day!" A smile usually gives me away as I drive off.

My all-time favorite short hair story, however, takes place in the women's bathroom. You know, the place with a lounge, big mirrors, and spotless appearance. Men usually haven't seen this place, so I like to embellish. Anyway, I'm standing at the sink, casually washing my hands. In the mirror, I see a woman enter the bathroom through the door behind me. Seeing my buzz cut, she freezes. Her eyes grow wide, her shoulders edge up to her ears, and the rest of her body goes stiff. Then, she lurches away, backpedaling over the tile floor, squeezing her body through the door. Still facing me, she leans out of the restroom to check the blue sign on the wall outside the door. She looks at me again. She leans back outside of the restroom, double checking the sign: WOMEN. Keeping an eye trained on the back of my head, she re-enters, hugging the wall of the restroom. She quickly finds her chosen stall, whips the door closed, and hits the lock. The thought of this woman still makes me laugh.

Another time, another bathroom, same scenario: a woman double checks the sign. I give her a big smile. She and her friend bust out in laughter and apologies. As I continue on with my day, scanning a Walmart shelf for oatmeal, an employee passes by the aisle, does a double-take and comes to chat with me. I learn all about him and his beloved mother. This guy and his mom each grew up here, outside Columbus, Georgia. *Well, I've got nothing better to do. Why not talk to him?* I start to share. "Let me tell you something funny that just happened in the women's restroom." At some point in the story, I reach up to touch my head. He checks out my bicep. The story ends as I tell him the women clearly thought I was male. He responds with a surprising inquiry, "Is that hereditary?" *What?* This time, I froze. "You mean, is looking like a dude hereditary? Yes. My brother and dad have the same affliction." In reality, that's not what I said to him. I'm sure I stammered something about cutting my hair for work.

2.

Why did you want to go to Ranger School?

This is where I tell you who I am. I grew up in Baltimore County, Maryland. The middle child in a family of five, born to two awesome entrepreneurs and globetrotters. My father taught me to give a firm handshake and look people in the eye. My mother showed me what it was to serve others. Growing up, my memories of my mother are of her working at the office, picking us kids up from activities, or making sure she was home by the time we returned from school. She was always doing something for someone else.

I didn't know much about the military. I visited the Naval Academy during high school, not knowing what it was. At the time, college brochures held zero appeal for me and my mother was starting to worry. On the visit, the tour guide showed us Olympic-size pools, red and black matted wrestling rooms, and the names of all graduates who died in service. He told visitors about the challenges each cadet had to overcome in order to graduate. The academy showed me that college could be about more than academics. An academy offered me the chance to grow both mentally and physically. It offered challenge and a life of service.

At the Naval Academy, the statues and buildings are named after ships. At West Point, they're named after people. This proved a great metaphor. The Army is about people, not ships or multimillion dollar systems. I chose to attend West Point to learn to lead *people*. As a cadet, I strove to be the best I could be. Sometimes, I took cadet life far too seriously. Other times, my drive helped me to take advantage of some incredible opportunities. I rowed crew for a semester, competed on the Sandhurst team, and competed as a member of the Sport Parachute Team.

Once, a classmate asked me, "If Ranger School was open to women, would you go?" I responded that it didn't matter because it *wasn't* open to women. The case was closed in my mind. Years later, when I was a newly commissioned second lieutenant, Ranger School started to toy with the idea of opening to women. At the time, I was getting ready for Sapper School, although I wouldn't have a shot at Sapper School for another three years. My first commander sent me to Ranger Training Assessment Course (RTAC) at Fort Benning in order for me to earn the chance to attend Ranger School. If successful, I would join the only Ranger class admitting women at the time, the pilot class. I was not successful, so I asked to attend RTAC again for one last shot at Ranger School. I failed the push-ups on the Ranger Phyiscal Fitness Test (RPFT). I thought I was ready to be a Ranger, yet I had failed a simple fitness test. I returned to my unit feeling ashamed. My unit, however, was proud. They were proud to have sent one of the 138 women who threw their hat in the ring for an attempt at Ranger School.

Ultimately, my RTAC failure lit a fire in me. I refused to let a school defeat me and decided that I would do whatever it took to conquer Ranger School.

Back at my unit, my soldiers provided motivation for me to do whatever it took to be a better leader, to be worthy of their loyalty. My unit was trained to perform subterranean rescue. However, it was difficult to find and gain access to underground training facilities. When we did find a reliable facility, the facility manager asked if, while we were in his tunnel, we could retrieve a broken fan. Hoping to return the good will of the facility manager, I directed a team of four soldiers to, if possible, retrieve the broken fan from the six-foot diameter drainage tunnel. The fan was a mile and a half into the tunnel. The soldiers were breathing through respirators and carrying oxygen tanks on their backs. Just two minutes before their two-hour time hack was complete, I could hear the team racing back to the tunnel entrance. They emerged into the daylight, splashing through the stream at their feet, each carrying equipment and pieces of the fan. They collapsed onto the stream bank, pulling off their respirators. They were exhausted and drenched in sweat. The fan they had removed from the wall of the tunnel and broken into pieces was massive. Just the outer rim of the metal, circular fan was easily three feet in diameter and three feet long. The soldier who had carried it out was barely five feet tall. As he sat on the stream bank, all you could see was his legs. He had carried the rim of the fan around his body, placing his hands at the bottom and allowing the rest of it to obscure his vision. He had been too exhausted to do anything other than sit down with fan still encasing his upper body. I had made a simple request, and these soldiers had given every ounce of effort to make sure they accomplished their task. This is just one small example of the effort and sacrifice soldiers make every day for their leaders, subordinates, and each other.

In 2016, my RTAC training paid dividends. The patrolling lessons I had learned helped me tab Sapper School. At Sapper School, 'heartbreak day' refers to the day students are told whether they graduated as Sappers, or recycle and re-do patrolling phase, or go to the house. My classmates and I sat in folding metal chairs at three rows of tables, in an unassuming stand-alone classroom. We were silent as the Commander, standing in front of the projection screen, read off our names. "Name: *recycle*… Name: *house*… Name: *Sapper*…McShane: *Sapper*." I was bursting with pride and gratitude.

A year later, as an instructor at Fort Leonard Wood, my new boss supported me in another attempt at Ranger School. I trained hard. Then, I failed push-ups again. I was ashamed, again. I called my commander, asking for one more chance. It was *deja vu*. I'd made the same phone call two years prior when I'd failed RTAC and asked for one more chance. "That's all I need," I told my new commander, **"one more chance at Ranger."** I hung up the phone and felt fear. I did not want to be wrong. I drove straight to the gym, Uncommon Athlete. The gym's head trainer gave me push-up programming and overall Ranger programming. When I had my second chance in the gates of Ranger School four weeks later, I breezed through the push-up event, finally. Students around me couldn't figure out why I was beaming with happiness: we hadn't even finished the RPFT. In my mind, I was finally in the game. I was in Ranger School.

In Darby Phase, I struggled with the steps of a Ranger School ambush and had to recycle. By Darby 'round two,' I had experience and confidence from having completed the phase once already. I also out-ranked and had more Army experience that the majority of my peers. The cadre put me in charge as student leadership for my company. In my Mountains patrol, equipment went missing. I took responsibility and recycled. No regrets. I was prepared to fail in Florida, but I passed.

All throughout Ranger School, one misstep threatened to end a student's Ranger School career—injury, patrol failure, uncontrollable circumstances. After that, the failed student would have to re-start the school if they wanted to tab. The final week was no different. "If you show up one minute after formation, you won't graduate," the instructor promised. After three months in school, I made it to graduation. I beamed, grateful for the presence of friends and family as my mother pinned on my Ranger tab. I walked away from graduation repeating like broken record, "*They can't take it from me anymore. They can't take it. They can't take it.*" For months, I had dedicated myself to graduating Ranger School, only to be reminded that one misstep could send me back to the start. Finally, it was over. They couldn't fail me now.

I knew my 'why.' I had many why's for attending Ranger

School: to be a better leader for my soldiers, (because I will never be good enough to deserve their incredible loyalty), to prove to myself that I could, to go through 'the suck,' and become better for it, to increase the number of women who had graduated and to defeat the negative stereotypes... because I could. And yet, there's a big part of my 'why' that I can't explain. There was intuition telling me to go to Ranger School, to do whatever it took, and to help others to do the same.

3.

How should I prepare for Ranger School? Is there anything specific (like upper body strength) I need to focus on?

Look, it's all about you: your strengths, your weaknesses, your plan. Personally, I had bad push-up form. That made push-ups a significant issue. There are many women and men for whom push-ups will never be an issue. One trend among friends and trainees who went to Ranger and Sapper Schools is that their failures occurred in those areas in which they were most confident. They were side swiped by challenges that they thought they had 'in the bag' and didn't need to train. Ranger Tactical Tasks (RTT's), land navigation, and push-ups, to name a few. There is one way to prevent this: external, expert feedback. Here's what's needed. First, a plan. Know the requirements, or gates, of Ranger School. These are the gates: RPFT, CWST, Malvesti Obstacle Course, RTT's, Land Navigation, 12-mile Ruck March, Patrols, and general ruck marching. Of these, if you can easily and calmly swim with a FLC and weapon and manage to not get injured or quit, then ignore the CWST and the Malvesti. Don't worry about training for these. People are not dropped from Ranger School for these events outside of the reasons listed above. I'm speaking in generalities here. Now then, take the remaining gates and your calendar. Plan out how and when you will become proficient in each: RPFT, RTT's, Land Navigation, 12-mile Ruck March, Patrols, general rucking. You know your weaknesses. That's where to place your focus, initially.

Within the first two weeks of starting your train-up, schedule an expert to provide feedback. At a minimum, this should be feedback on push-ups, pull-ups, and weapons-related RTT's. This feedback allows you to recognize weaknesses that you didn't identify previously in order to address them before they lead to failure. Who counts as an expert? For RTT's, experts include former Ranger Instructors or an infantryman who is intimately familiar with Expert Infantryman Badge (EIB) standards. For push-ups and pull-ups, Ranger Instructors are the experts. Second best is someone who struggled on these events, then passed, because they were forced to learn the details of how Ranger Instructors grade in order to improve, then pass. Of course, any expert has to be able to give honest feedback.

After doing a practice RPFT and gaining corrections on the RTT's, it's time to adjust the plan to account for newly identified weaknesses. In this new plan, schedule at least one more session to receive expert feedback on push-ups, pull-ups, and weapons-related RTT's.

Within the last 30 days before entering Ranger School,

fine tune your RTT skills and get on a land navigation course. More specifically, get your handson weapons systems 2-3 times per week and repeatedly perform each RTT to standard. For land navigation, remember that it is a perishable skill. It needs to be practiced in order to maintain competency. During these final 30 days, choose a challenging course that requires more than just terrain association to pass. Practice all the tools in your toolbox: terrain association, azimuths, cloverleaf, backstops, utilizing pace count, etc. By using multiple tools in practice and on Ranger School's course, any error in navigation can be quickly remedied by using an alternate tool to confirm location.

You might be wondering, "Hey, where's the female-specific aspect of this training guidance?" There is none. "What about upper body strength?" Well, can you do 49+ push-ups in two minutes and 6+ pull-ups to the Ranger standard? The way to train for Ranger School (and any other school for that matter) is to look at the defined requirements. Measure yourself against those requirements and train for those requirements. The perfect plan for you is not a general women's training plan, but a plan designed to address your weaknesses in the specific areas in which you will be tested. General upper body strength training is good, but may or may not be necessary or specific enough for you based on your ability to perform the push-up and pull-up events and the amount of time you have to train.

Training for Ranger is different from training for Delta or Special Forces selection. For more info on the need to train for your specific school or sport, listen to this podcast with Rob Shaul of Mountain Tactical Athlete 38:20 https://www.artofmanliness.com/articles/podcast-270-becoming-tactical-athlete. The question is not, "I'm a woman, am I capable?" Instead, ask yourself, "Am I capable? Can I perform each of the requirements?" If not, train to be able to pass that requirement. If your push-ups need work, then, at that point, look at your movement patterns. These movement patterns are unique to you, but may be comparable more to women or men. Women tend to recruit different muscles for some exercises, but this is not a rule. When it comes to pull-ups, I rely mostly on biceps (similar to many women) while my female roommate recruits almost strictly back muscles (similar to many men). Our respective programming for improvement are different.

Outside of physical preparation, it is important to prepare for patrols. Still, it is far more important to focus on training for RAP week than for patrolling. Why? Ranger School does not allow anyone to recycle RAP week. At the same time, nearly 50% of all Ranger students are dropped during this week. In effect, there is little room for error when it comes to RAP week events. Patrols, however, have a backstop. After RAP week is complete and the focus shifts to patrols, students are given the opportunity to recycle. Each student is given two leadership attempts in order to pass patrols. If someone fails both attempts, they can recycle and get two more in their second round of Darby. I'm not saying don't train for patrols. I'm saying don't try to perfect your operations order when you haven't had an expert test your RPFT and RTT's. When you do practice patrols, get a squad-size element together and rehearse every single step that Ranger School publishes for Ambush, React to Contact, and Crossing a Linear Danger Area. There are other patrols and battle drills you will be expected to execute. However, if you walk through these three with friends before entering the school, you'll create a mental model of what they need to look like when executed. This will be a fantastic foundation to help you more easily learn the rest of the patrols and battle drills graded at Ranger School.

If you can already complete an ambush, good. Be aware that Darby phase of Ranger demands that you learn and execute each patrol and battle drill according to their list of specific steps, as they teach them. It may seem odd to complete an Ambush as a checklist. Still, that is expectation. To see Ranger School's steps for completing an Ambush, see Ranger Training Brigade's published video on an Ambush according to Ranger School's steps: http://www.benning.army.mil/INFANTRY/ARTB/Student-Information/Videos.html. To see Ranger's steps for React to Contact, Crossing a Linear Danger Area, other battle drills, and RTT's, see the Ranger School Training App created by Upper Tier Development: https://play.google.com/store/apps/details?id=com.uppertierdevelopment.rangerpro&hl=en_US.

4.

Are the standards the same?

Good Lord. It that still a question? I was speaking to command teams on Fort Leonard Wood and a well-meaning 1SG asked me this question. *YES. The standards are the same for every Soldier who walks in the gate.* Take the RPFT as the first example. All students stand in a large formation wearing uniforms and sporting identical haircuts. When the Ranger students who are 'next in line' for the RPFT are called, they run over to the wood-chip pit to perform the push-up event. There is no score card to fill out with the annotation, M or F in the gender box. It's just you and your grader. Once the required 49 push-ups are complete, the student is sent to either the failure and re-test formation, or the pass formation. No one gives a shit about gender. If they do, they are too professional to say anything.

What about patrols? By the time you are in patrols, your grader has probably figured out your sex. At that point, you either lead a good patrol, or you don't. There is subjectivity in grading patrols. There has to be. The graders have a defined checklist to determine whether a student is a GO or NO-GO. However, it is up to them whether the student appeared confident and in control or dazed and confused. I don't know specifically what is on those grading sheets, but none of the items on the checklist have anything to do with gender.

If the standards were different, many women would refuse to go to the school. It would cheapen the Ranger tab. From the time the pilot class was first considered, leaders and candidates alike echoed the same sentiment: maintain the same standards for all soldiers.

5.

What was your Army Physical Fitness Test score as a cadet?

I don't recall the score. It was likely around 280. I tended to slowly lower myself to the ground during the sit-up, fighting rather than using gravity. During my basic officer course, I focused on improving push-ups and sit-ups. I have maxed each record APFT since. My last PT test before RTAC, I completed 64 push-ups in two minutes. I then trained a deeper push-up in an effort to prepare for the RPFT. During my first RPFT, instead of 64, the RTAC grader counted only 24 push-ups. There it was, overconfidence in push-ups got the better of me. It took me two years and four more RPFT push-up attempts at RTAC and Ranger before I finally realized that doing 1000's of push-ups wasn't fixing the problem. I finally requested and received expert, external feedback and great programming from Uncommon Athlete, a gym in Columbus, Georgia. By dropping my ego and following their guidance, I finally passed the RPFT.

6.

What was it like being the only woman at Ranger School?

Pretty normal, actually. The Army is generally a male-dominated environment and nothing seemed out of character. Admittedly, there were certain odd parts. My first time through the gates, I followed the guidance that, according to AR 670-1, women were authorized to cut their hair to ¼ inch and no shorter. The men shaved their heads to the scalp until their hair felt like Velcro. With more hair than everyone else, I stood out like a sore thumb. Really, I stood out like a costumed duck at a 007-themed Halloween party. My hair was a beacon. See for yourself, watch this Ranger School video and tell me whether or not your attention is drawn to the long haircuts. https://www.youtube.com/watch?v=wvxqxylAyE0. My second time in the gate, after seeing this video, my head felt like Velcro.

Going to Ranger School, I hadn't known what to expect. Would there be differences because I was a woman? Were the cadre going to give me hell? In fact, being a woman was a *non-issue*. How incredible. Hats off to Ranger School. From 2015 to 2017 they had overcome external and internal resistance and ensured everyone was treated as a soldier. In less than two years, they had integrated women to the point that being a woman in the course was a non-issue.

In high school, I spent my summers working on the high ropes course at a Boy Scout camp in Maryland. One summer, out of 80 or so camp staff, there were two women. In college, my West Point class was around 83% male, 17% women. The majority of my friends were men. My first squad was all men, save for me. Most times, I don't notice the ratio. I love the Army and appreciate the environment for what it is.

Entering Ranger school, I did have one concern: I was concerned that, because I was a woman, perhaps I would be more emotional than my classmates. Instead, I learned that Ranger School is an emotional place for many. I saw man tears, fear of failure, and more victim mentality than I'd ever expected. There were times when I was more emotional than others; there were times when I reassured an emotional teammate.

The one oddity was in the showers. When women first arrived at Ranger School in 2015, showers caused some drama. The Ranger Instructors mandated that women could not shower unless there were two instructors standing guard, one at either door. They also mandated that everyone take showers before going to sleep. When students were released to the barracks to shower and sleep, the instructors were nowhere to be found. Therefore, after a long day with just three hours for shut eye before the next challenge, no one could sleep because the women needed to shower. It was the little inconveniences that made women unwelcome. Thanks to some powerful influencers, that trend disappeared well before I arrived at Ranger School. When I attended, students were responsible for managing themselves. There were guidelines regarding student guards during female shower time during RAP week and Darby. Honestly, I ignored those. I was keen on avoiding any inconvenience that might convince a student that they'd prefer not to have women around.

During RAP week, once the guard rule was ignored, showering was easy. There were single stall showers with white plastic curtains. I changed, showered, and changed again behind the privacy of a curtain. No need to draw attention to myself. In Darby phase, women were told to shower first. I ran and took the shortest shower possible, doing most re-dressing outside the bathroom. In Mountain Phase, round one, there were open bay showers. As soon as we returned to the barracks, I would race to grab my shower gear from my locker, get a 3-minute shower, and get out so that the men wouldn't have to wait their turn because the showers would already be open for them. In Mountain Phase, round two, the shower routine changed. I transferred my curtain to the upstairs shower, where two women in separate companies would be taking their showers. I was still intent on preventing any inconvenience for my classmates, but less concerned about privacy. In Mountains, round two, I'd wait until what seemed like a less popular shower time. Then, shower gear in hand, I'd approach the showers and shout a question, "Is anyone offended if a female enters the shower? Ok, you're about to be starship-troopered." (I never got through the book, but in the movie, Starship Troopers, there is a shower scene where soldiers, male and female alike, talk and joke in open bay showers.) Nudity is a non-issue. And although I've never been naked in France, I've heard that they are far more laissez faire on the topic. The fact that nudity is so taboo is a cultural phenomenon. Anyway, when men are at the urinal, they typically give one another space and don't sneak peaks. That is how I treated the shower. I kept my eyes to myself and hoped the others did the same. If there was a perv in the group, that was their problem. I knew the guys in my company. We were all on the same team. In no way did I feel at risk. I suppose this is true integration. By the time Florida phase arrived, however, I was tired of setting the norms on showers with new groups of people. I asked our class leader if I could hit the shower a few minutes before our 'no earlier than' shower time. I was out of the way before others needed the shower space.

7.

As a woman, what strengths did you have to offer that the men didn't?

I hate this question. I know where it comes from. Women are tired of hearing that 'women don't belong' in Ranger School or anywhere else. Arguing with bigotry is frustrating. Not that all who question women's role in Ranger School are bigots, some people just adopt bigot notions. In response, some women want the ultimate show-stopper, the one statement that will win the argument once and for all. I don't win that way. Despite writing a book, I am more apt to trip over my words when excited by this argument than to respond intelligently with the perfect come-back. Believe me, in college I tried to win the argument on why small-minded ideas were ridiculous. The conversation would start in frustration and end with more frustration. Words and argument have never been my battle ground. Instead, I've learned to do nothing. I just show up. People change their minds about whatever sexist notion they harbored or considered harboring when they work with me. I show up and do what I always do: work hard and try to do the right thing. I'm sure I don't change everyone's mind, but it's always a nice surprise when someone approaches me after a field exercise and says, "Hey, McShane. Before we went into the field, I didn't know what I thought about women in the Infantry. But after this, I'm cool with it. You killed it out there."

It's a blessing to live in this day and age. I will forever be grateful to the women of times past, especially women of the 80s. My mentor and friend, Mrs. Kris Fuhr, was a cadet in the 6th West Point class to admit women. There were blatant, repeated, and ignored sexual assaults, including rape. In the absence of door locks, Kris and her roommate propped a dustpan against the door every night, in hopes that its fall would wake them in time to defend themselves. I can only imagine the fear they lived with. See her video for yourself, http://www.westpointcoh.org/interviews/locking-shields-surviving-west-point-as-a-woman. It's thanks to people like Kris that being a woman in today's Army, even Ranger School, is a non-issue. She dealt with atrocities that I will never fully appreciate. In my world, to overcome sexism, I don't have to fight, I just have to be me.

What strengths do women bring to the table? We bring our strengths to the table as individuals, not as a gender. Every individual has personal strengths; we also develop skills based on our environment and the needs of our team. Personally, I'm an optimist, I share positivity even when the going gets rough. In Ranger School, we constantly learn new, useful skills. When recycling, I could remember the value provided by past recycles and remember gaps in team performance during the last phase. Not all of those lessons apply to the new group, so the ultimate question is, 'What does my team need?' Perhaps operations orders are vague. Or, there's a machine gun that needs carried and operated. Does this squad leader need a good team leader? Is there additional equipment that needs carried? Perhaps people need someone to walk them through crew drills. If the Platoon Leader is lost in the planning process, they need good planners and someone to orient them to their most critical tasks. As you go along, you add more skills to your repertoire. You are more prepared to be a better team player and offer your strengths for your team. I was a much better teammate after each recycle because I had a better understanding of what was needed. I had more useful skills by virtue of having gone through the phase before.

In an effort to answer in a women-specific fashion, perhaps some men were more comfortable opening up and sharing an emotional struggle with me. But really, even that's a stretch.

Serving Food

As I fell into my first formation in Mountain phase, a recycle helped orient the squad. He let us know what to expect during Mountain phase. "You get a hot meal in the cafeteria every morning, but not much time to eat it. In the field, we get one meal a day; in classroom phase, we get three." *What?* Three meals a day? Hot breakfast every morning? This sounded like the best phase ever. Sure enough, breakfast was fantastic. As the reader, you probably wouldn't be too impressed, but to an emaciating Ranger Student, pancakes, cereal, a side of cake, eggs, sausage, bread, and a milk carton was a feast. A daily feast. When breakfast time came, students were given serving duties. Duties included opening the door, controlling the wait line, handing out plates of food, and handing out drinks. The worst job was the 'table Nazi.' This student ensured that everyone with a tray of food could sit down and eat. Therefore, they also dictated who was done eating and needed to leave their table. Each student had approximately 5-8 minutes to eat. If the table Nazi was good at their job, students had more time to eat.

If you weren't on duty, it was your job to take hints from the table Nazi in an attempt maximize everyone's breakfast time and to eat as fast as possible. When you ate quickly, you could eat more. It's like that one saying, "You don't have to outrun the bear, you just have to outrun your buddy." You don't have to be the fastest eater, but it pays to eat faster than your buddy. If you ate faster than the person next to you, they would realize time was up and throw their extra food your way. I became pretty good at shoveling food. As a side note, one of my squad mates realized that I preferred not to eat the cake and would trade it for anything. He would sit by me and make the silent trade. Meanwhile, I was dipping bread in milk. Soggy bread is ingested in seconds, way faster than chewing, adding saliva and choking down dry bread. I could usually scarf down my plate and more than a few sides my classmates threw my way. Every bit of extra food counted as a victory for the day. I'd walk out of the mess hall grinning from ear to ear, thinking of all the extra food I'd scored.

Even more satisfying than winning extra food was serving. When on mess hall duty, I always volunteered to hand out plates of food. In spite of my enthusiasm for breakfast, I noticed that not everyone woke up happy. Many students walked to the food line with their head down, contemplating whatever challenge stood before them. One benefit of recycling was that I knew quite a few of them. "Hey, John. It's great to see you. What's going on?" John would pick his head up, smile back, and connect with me. Even if I didn't know the person, "Hey, man. Good to see you." Or just, "Enjoy breakfast." A couple people responded with a grimace. The vast majority, however, forgot whatever they had been ruminating on. Especially for my friends, I helped bring some light into their days and helped them to enjoy their breakfasts just a little bit more.

8.

Were your peers resistant to your leadership?

I experienced zero sexism at Ranger School. I was incredibly grateful and impressed with how times had changed. There may well have been side conversations in other companies while I attended Ranger School. However, as soon as anyone got near me, sharing either a squad, platoon, or company, they realized I was an asset to the team. I think it's easier for sexism to thrive in an office setting than in the field. In the field, your team is everything. Your team members rely on one another. You learn quickly who you can rely on, who you can trust, and what you can expect from each person. Those who work hard, build their competence, and have your back are invaluable, and you know who they are. I was reliable. When my teammates were in a tough spot, time was short, and they needed something, someone had let them down, they knew they could count on me. In Mountain Phase, one student failed to complete a manifest roster for the Platoon Sergeant. The Platoon Sergeant came to ask me to take over the task. On another patrol, the Platoon Leader blanked when it came time to set up a patrol base. He asked for help and I organized each team in the order in which they needed to enter the patrol base. On the final Florida patrol, a Platoon Leader needed a good operations order to get his GO. He asked for me. In turn, I assembled a team of people whom I could trust to help create a quality product. My actions for others were not remarkable, they were necessary. No one gets their GO alone. We all supported and relied one another to achieve success.

9.

Which was harder, Sapper or Ranger? What was the hardest part?

The hardest days were in Sapper School. Boat physical training (Boat PT) and the Sapper long walk are two experiences I never want to go through again. They were each harder than any single aspect of Ranger School.

On the day of Boat PT, we woke up long before the sun and assembled next to our Zodaics boats, inflatable black boats weighing over 300 lbs. each. Though we only had a mile to carry them and six soldiers to a boat, the instructors ensured that every inch of that mile was painful. They stood on top of the boats, yelling for us to pick up and put it down, overhead-press the boat, and do a number of terrible exercises.

Though no single event in Ranger School ever compared to Sapper's Boat PT or its long walk, Ranger School is hard because of the endurance required. Ranger School is months long. Month after month with little food and little sleep take a mental toll.

10.

What mental strategies did you use?

It's because I've been asked this question that I now recognize and name some of the strategies I used. Many of these strategies are probably already familiar to you: see the positive side of everything, someone always has it worse, tired is an attitude, and it's not whether you can, it's whether you *choose* to.

Seeing the positive side of everything

People complain a lot. Is it because we're the entitled generation? Maybe, but I doubt it. My own father complains about plenty of petty things, but he's made it in this world and he can afford to differentiate between what he expects and what he doesn't like. Ranger students like to complain about the cold, the lack of food, the push-ups, and the lack of sleep. I have a personal rule: never complain. Things could *always* be worse and you always have a better lot than someone else. At Ranger School though, I broke my own rule. It happened in the second round of Mountain phase. It was cold and dark, I was hungry and tired. I found my squad mate who chronically complained and told him,

"Fuck, it's cold." His reply, "I know, man!" was almost enthusiastic. We spent the next mile or so talking about hunger, the contents of our unopened MRE's (Meals Ready to Eat), and how we planned to eat them. "I've been saving this one," he said. "It's my favorite MRE and I think we'll be given a few more minutes to eat tonight." That was the best bonding session he and I ever had.

In Darby phase, people would complain or be bitter about getting 'smoked.' They would be bitter, either at the instructors, or the students who seemed to draw the instructors' wrath on all of us. What we hadn't realized at the time, is that a good portion of these 'smoke sessions' are literally on the schedule. 0715: Smoke students for lack of hustle. 0830: Smoke students for failure to meet an unreasonable time hack. Actually, the 'smoking' was good for us. No, I am not being masochistic or overly hard core. The instructors used fear of pain (push-ups, Y-squats, whatever) to motivate students to move faster. We learned to pack rucks in seconds, to run, and to finish a task rather than drag ass. By the time we were patrolling, everyone knew how to hustle. Everyone knew how to get shit done quickly. We could pack our gear in the morning and move out in time to arrive on the objective in daylight. People could conduct required tasks quickly, so we could get more shut eye. By recycling Darby, I experienced one company which smoked us a lot, and one which smoked us very little. I preferred the first company, the one that smoked us a lot; that's because it translated into better discipline and better patrols. In the second company, you'd tell a slow-ass soldier,

"Hurry up, just shove that shit in your ruck." He'd reply, "I am hurrying!" as he made sure everything was neatly organized. His lack of hustle prevented the team from stepping off early in order to get to the objective while there was still daylight. One soldier was dragging ass and it was now a problem for the whole team. He hadn't learned through pain and now it was your job to teach him to hustle. In other words, there's a positive side to 'getting smoked.' Keep that in mind when the instructors smoke you and threaten to get under your skin.

Also, keep in mind that each phase of Ranger School prepares you for the next. In terms of rucking, Mountain rucks in the winter are the heaviest, between 75 and 120 pounds. My fire support officer's ruck (typically one of the heaviest in the platoon) weighed in at 114 lbs. Don't let 114 or 120 scare you. Train with 60 lbs. so as not to break yourself in training before even arriving to Benning. In Darby phase, you will carry your ruck with you everywhere, during classroom days and patrolling. Darby conditions you to carry the weight. By the time you get to Mountain phase, you're ready for it. If a ruck feels heavy in Darby, just remember, this is conditioning you for Mountains. You CAN carry the rucks in Mountains. The more weight you carry here, the easier the rucks will feel there. A heavy ruck is just good training.

Avoid victim mentality at all costs. Victim mentality occurs when people decide that this school COULD defeat them. They are afraid of failing and consumed by this fear. Don't get me wrong, no-one wants to fail and a level of fear and self-doubt is normal. The problem occurs when people fail to do what's needed and they take actions harmful to their team because they are focused on self-preservation. I watched as all but two riflemen in a platoon hid in the crowd when instructed to pick up empty water jugs to carry on their ruck during the upcoming movement. They were either too lazy or too worried about the impact of carrying a completely empty water jug to do the simple task. With this focus on self-preservation, any extra weight in their ruck could weaken them for the next day and prevent them from getting a GO. Any extra task, like running the trash to the dumpster, is expending energy that needs to be saved. That's fear talking or sheer laziness. It certainly is not the Ranger mentality of giving 'one-hundred-percent and then some.' Avoid victim mentality at all costs. You always have more energy and you can always do more than you think you can.

It's not whether you can, it's whether you choose to

My hardest day at any Army school was the day of the Sapper School Long Walk. It started after a demolition mission. Of course, the instructors said that much of the (fake) demolition failed to detonate and had to be carried. There were 40 lb. cratering charges, shape charges, and assorted other demolition collected in two piles on the road. Everyone stood, rucks open on either side of those piles. People kept calling for more bodies to grab more demolition. I went back to the pile two, three times, grabbing more for my ruck. When I finally put it on and started walking, fear hit me. *Oh God. I may not make it.* This was the first ruck I had ever carried that made me question whether I could make it a mile, let alone the 15 estimated miles ahead of us. My focus narrowed, my thoughts kept reverting back to their new default: I don't know if I can make it. At one point, I remembered that one of the dudes in my squad was a chronic slacker. He and I were on good terms, but he hadn't exactly made friends in Sapper School. Four miles in, the Platoon Leader called a 'halt' and instructed his subordinates to make any adjustments needed. Although that dude was a slacker, he had proven to be a stronger rucker than I was. I convinced him to give me his ruck for the next leg and take mine, loaded as it was with a 40 lb. cratering charge, and whatever other demo. When he picked it up, his exclamation let me know that he was not so happy with our trade anymore. When I picked up his ruck, I discovered he had been slacking when we were loading our rucks with demo. This felt like justice. Also gratitude. He helped me out, big time.

Fifteen miles turned into eighteen miles of heavy rucks, receiving contact, then carrying casualties and their rucks on top of what we were already carrying. We finished the movement drenched in sweat, covered in grime and sorer than we'd thought possible. We were exhausted and it was time for our next mission. One of my friends was given a squad leader position. She needed team leaders. She asked for volunteers. I thought, "I am wrecked right now. I can't be the good team leader she needs." I didn't volunteer. She failed that mission and recycled the phase. I'm not saying that I caused her failure or that I would have been the team leader she needed to get her GO. I am saying that I was wrong. When she recycled the phase, I knew I'd let her down. I know now that it was not a question of whether I could be the team leader she needed. It was whether I CHOSE to be the team leader she needed. No matter how tired, how hungry, how hurt I may be, I know that I can always step up. I can choose to overcome my circumstances and do what needs to be done. THAT is what being a Sapper or a Ranger is all about.

"Readily will I display the intestinal fortitude required to fight on to the Ranger objective and complete the mission, though I be the lone survivor." —Ranger Creed

No matter the conditions, I need to be there for my teammates, to give one hundred percent, and then some, and accomplish the mission. I learned my lesson, I learned to be there for my Ranger teammates in a way that I wasn't there for my Sapper teammate.

Someone always has it worse

This complements the idea of never complaining. It's best applied when we want to feel sorry for ourselves or take an easy way out. Knees hurt in Ranger School. Any halt longer than a few seconds demands that every individual take a knee and pull security. As the team gets closer to the patrol base, no one wants to take a knee. My first round in Darby, I was pulling security, thinking about my knees. I had switched my weight from one knee to the next, and back again. I was considering standing or sitting down. "Just for a second," I justified. Right then, my squad mate took a knee next to me, sharing a tree for cover. "Hey, man," I say. I mention that Ranger School is rough on the knees. "Yeah, dude. My knee is killing me too." Then I remembered, he had cellulitis. One of his knees was the size of a grapefruit. He was only using one knee to kneel, taking twice as much pressure to that one knee than I was to mine. So much for sitting down. He was still doing the right thing. I would too.

You never know what someone is carrying in their rucksack. If someone is struggling, they may be carrying more weight than you, physically or mentally. They may be hiding an injury. They may have family issues they're dealing with on top of dealing with Ranger requirements. If you think you're struggling, think of others. Someone needs this school to get promoted and put food on the table for their family. You can step it up for them.

Tired is an attitude

One day, in Darby phase, I woke up in the morning after maybe an hour of sleep. "Oh no," I thought, "I am so tired. How am I going to get any more sleep today?" Of course, I wasn't. There are no Ranger siestas. I was devastated, thinking of how it was going to be such a struggle to get through the day. That turned out to be a great day. Instructors led us through ambush rehearsals. It was sunny, warm, and I already had a 'warm and fuzzy' on Ambush: this was Darby round two after all. I spent the rehearsals helping my buddies learn and, when I was stuck on security, too far away to hear the Ranger instructor, my buddy and I enjoyed swapping stories and asking questions about home. It occurred to me that I had just as much sleep at the time that I was loving life, swapping stories with my buddy as I did when I woke up feeling sorry for myself. Tired is an attitude. After realizing this, I had zero issues waking up during Ranger School. I woke up, climbed out of the sleeping bag, and immediately set to work, packing up equipment and completing all necessary tasks.

Back at home now, I do indulge my snooze button every so often. However, when there is a task or goal in front of me, I deliberately train myself to wake up immediately with my alarm. Part of this training is to block thoughts. It's the thoughts that make waking up difficult. I can avoid negative thoughts by immediately getting up and doing something habitual, like brushing teeth, then accomplishing whatever tasks are needed to get me out the door.

11.

Do I tell people I'm going to Ranger School?

Okay, no one has actually asked me this question. This is my own plug. If you are reading this book in preparation for Ranger School, then, most likely, you are willing to do what it takes to get to Ranger School. I recommend being honest. When it comes up in conversation, don't avoid telling people that you want to attend Ranger School. I am speaking mostly to women on this one. No one wants to be 'that guy.' The one who talked a big game, but ultimately counted their chickens before they hatched. In this case, no one wants to claim that they're ready to be a Ranger, only to fail push-ups. Been there. However, if you refrain from saying you want to go to Ranger School, you are preventing people from being able to support you. You also are shying away from an opportunity to be a positive example. When I was getting ready to attend Ranger School, there were zero, then three, then seven female Ranger graduates. People didn't know women graduates. They didn't know women who even wanted to attend. By being honest about what you want, you can be the example for others of what a high-speed soldier and potential female graduate looks like. As your friends encounter small minds and those who don't think women should be able to attend Ranger School, you can be their example as they fight the good fight.

Epilogue

I want to applaud the Ranger Training Brigade. Their mission is a vital one. Integration, at first, seemed to take attention away from their vital mission. When it came time to integrate, many people inside and outside the organization were dead set against allowing women to join the infantry or to enter Ranger School. This sentiment was echoed at RTAC. There, instructors would conclude a class with their soliloquy on why mere presence of women would be the downfall of the infantry. Of course, the matter then became a topic of student discussion. It was a distraction that got in the way of training soldiers.

When the first 19 women entered Ranger School, women had to deal with resentment from instructors and classmates. Some of this was engineered resentment when women had to shower first with instructors guarding the doors, then instructors wouldn't show up, so no one got to shower or sleep. If you speak to an aviator that flew for Ft. Benning's airborne school at that time, they'll tell you that many Ranger graduates attend Airborne school immediately after Ranger School. They'll also tell you that those graduates who had been in the same class with the first women, were the most ragged, physically destroyed Ranger graduates they'd ever seen. Instructors, at least some, did not want women to pass. Great credit goes to the women who graduated under those conditions. More credit goes to the leadership that changed conditions from what they were to what they are today. Today, being a woman in Ranger School is a non-issue. We are all treated as soldiers. Ultimately, leadership said, "Enough is enough. I don't care that you're upset with women being here. They're here and that's that." They addressed the issues associated with discrimination. All instructors are on the same page, everyone is to be treated the same.

69391316R00033

Made in the USA
Columbia, SC
19 August 2019